HERO Likes Rea[ding]
But READING is Hard

by
Keith Magee

Illustrated by
Creative Graphics
India

HERO LIKES READING BUT READING IS HARD

Copyright © by Keith Magee

Illustration © by

Creative Graphics, India

Language Editors

Joanne Clay and Edward Weston

For more information

www.4JusticeSake.org

ISBN:

PoD Paperback: 978-1-915351-31-9
PoD hardback: 978-1-915351-32-6
eBook: 978-1-915351-33-3

Publisher:

Dolman Scott, 1 High Street, Thatcham, RG19 3JG, United Kingdom

HEREIN IS WRITTEN

In memory of Harry Belafonte

"MR B"

(1927 – 2023)

Hero likes running and playing with his friends.

He likes climbing trees with his brothers.

2

He likes running races with his mom too.

3

He likes playing games with his uncle.

4

But for Hero, reading is hard.

Hero likes going on long walks.

6

He likes walking by the river.

7

He likes walking to school.

He likes learning at school too.

But for Hero, reading is hard.

10

Hero likes
amusement
parks.

He likes art and music.

He likes math and science.

He likes singing and acting too.

But for Hero, reading is hard.

Hero likes going to the zoo.

16

He likes going to the aquarium.

He likes going to the planetarium.

He likes going to museums too.

But for Hero, reading is hard.

Hero likes reading about divers.

He likes reading about explorers.

He likes reading about racing-car drivers.

He likes reading about basketball too.

Hero is very fast.

26

He is very creative.

Hero is very clever.

He is very adventurous too.

For Hero reading is hard, but he loves practising!

Author's Note

"Where you begin

Doesn't determine

Where you end!"

Hero is inspired by the late actor, singer, and activist Harry Belafonte – better known as "Mr B" – who was a great advocate for children with reading difficulties. Hero represents all dyslexic children. Mr B saw dyslexia not as a disability but as a gift – he called it a 'superpower.'

One of Hero's favorite hobbies is reading, despite the fact he finds it hard. Hero enjoys lots of other activities too and has many great qualities in addition to his perseverance with reading.

All the other characters in the book are childhood versions of real-life famous people who are or were dyslexic. For each of them their dyslexia gives them a superpower, represented by something they are wearing or an object they have. As well as providing details about the places Hero visits, the list on pages 16–19 includes descriptions of each character's remarkable achievements. These mini-biographies show dyslexia is not a barrier to success, and are intended for adults to share with young readers, who may enjoy spotting the identifying clues in the illustrations.

May every dyslexic child beam with hope from reading this book. And may all readers – whether they are dyslexic or not find their inner strength to be and their own special superpower.

–Keith Magee

Hero

Hero represents all dyslexic children. Dyslexia is not Hero's disability as a gift –it a 'superpower.' The character is inspired by the late actor, singer, and activist Hero – better known as "Mr B" – who was a great advocate for children with reading difficulties.

Roberto Bolaño

A critically acclaimed Chilean author, poet, and essayist, Roberto Bolaño, is considered one of the great voices in modern Latin American literature. Ironically, Roberto, who was dyslexic, was also a prodigious reader as a child. He eventually left high school to pursue poetry and politics.

Carol Moseley Braun

A native of Chicago, Illinois, Carol Moseley Braun is the first African American woman elected to the US Senate, as well as a former US Ambassador and a lawyer. She has often said that her experience as a child with dyslexia fueled her determination to succeed and her political interest in education.

Princess Beatrice of York

The first-born child of Prince Andrew, Duke of York and Sarah Ferguson, Princess Beatrice, is the fifth grandchild of the late Queen Elizabeth II and Prince Philip. Beatrice was diagnosed with dyslexia at age seven. The princess, whose husband is also dyslexic, has described dyslexia as a "gift" that any child of hers would be "lucky" to have, saying "I think life is about the moments, it's the challenges that make you."

Crown Prince Carl Philip

The fourth in line to the Swedish throne, Crown Prince Carl Philip is the only son of King Carl XVI Gustaf and Queen Silvia. The prince publicly acknowledged his struggle with dyslexia after being ridiculed for mispronouncing someone's name during an award ceremony. He and his wife Princess Sofia have established a foundation to help those with learning disabilities and to combat cyber-bullying.

Danny Glover

Danny Glover is an American actor, film director, and political activist. His struggle with dyslexia began at an early age. Glover has often spoken about the lack of support available for a dyslexic child in the 1950s. He spends part of his time talking with students about overcoming obstacles.

Sir Richard Branson

Sir Richard Charles Nicholas Branson is a billionaire entrepreneur and founder of The Virgin Group which controls 400 businesses, including Virgin Atlantic Airways and the Virgin Voyages cruise line. He is quoted as saying: "Being dyslexic can actually help in the outside world. I see some things clearer than other people do because I have to simplify things to help me and that has helped others."

Karen Pritzker

A documentary film producer, investor, and philanthropist, Karen Pritzker was also an undiagnosed dyslexic. She executive produced *The Big Picture: Rethinking Dyslexia*, a documentary that demystified dyslexia and generated widespread awareness of this misunderstood disability. The film, which also won the Parents' Choice Award, continues to be screened all over the world, acting as a starting point for conversation and change.

Pablo Picasso

Spanish artist Pablo Ruiz Picasso was one of the most influential artists of the 20th century and a co-founder of the Cubist art movement. His artwork often presented objects seemingly out of order. But it is thought that his dyslexia would flip the orientation of letters and words in his brain. Picasso rendered what he saw, and his dyslexia was undoubtedly an influence on his artwork.

Centennial Park, Sydney, Australia

Centennial Park is the largest urban park in the southern hemisphere. Rich in history, the land was once the home of the Gadi people and was later the site of the signing of the Federation of Australia. Today it is Sydney's playground, offering acres of wide-open spaces for recreation, learning and leisure.

In Australia, 1 in 10 individuals has a learning disability. Eight in 10 individuals with learning disabilities have dyslexia. This equates to at least 2 million Australians with dyslexia.(https://dystech.com.au/education/the-economic-impact-of-dyslexia)

Royal River Thames, London

The Thames, as we commonly know it, is the longest river entirely within England and the second longest in the entire United Kingdom. The river is a historically important trade route that passes through London on its way to the sea.
In the United Kingdom an estimated 6.7 million people (around 10% of the population) have dyslexia. 1 in 6 adults has the reading level of an 11-year-old. (https://www.bdadyslexia.org.uk/)

Bayou of Louisiana

The word bayou originates from the Choctaw word "bayok," or small stream, which French immigrants translated into "bayouque." Over thousands of years the Mississippi River created the Louisiana Bayous, also sometimes called swamps. These wetlands may seem stagnant but the slow moving waters are full of seafood and wildlife and have been a home to native tribes and immigrants for centuries.

In the United States an estimated 15% of people have dyslexia, over 40 million adults. Between 5% and 12% of children have dyslexia in the US. Most students with dyslexia are not diagnosed until 3rd grade or later.
(Dyslexia Statistics, Facts and Figures (dyslexia-reading-well.com)

Page 9

Classroom in India

In ancient times, India had the Gurukula system of education. Anyone who wished to study went to a teacher's or guru's house and requested to be taught. If accepted, the student would then stay at the guru's place and help with all activities in the home. Now, India has the second-largest school system in the world. In 2001, the Indian government started a program called Sarva Shiksha Abhiyan to educate all children between the ages of 6 and 14.

Around 15% of all students enrolled in Indian schools are thought to have dyslexia.

Page 11

Walt Disney

Walter Elias "Walt" Disney was an American film producer, director, screenwriter, voice actor, animator, and motion picture producer. Many people believe that Mickey Mouse is his alter-ego. Although he dropped out of school at 15, Walt Disney went on to found and create both Disneyland and Disney World. Many scholars believe he that had dyslexia.

Page 12

Ludwig van Beethoven

No-one knows for certain, but it is widely believed that Beethoven was dyslexic because he had difficulties in school and often transposed letters and numbers. Beethoven published his first composition when he was 12 years old. When he was older, he is reported to have said that "music comes to me more readily than words."

Page 13

Dr. Maggie Aderin-Pocock

Margaret Ebunoluwa "Maggie" Aderin-Pocock MBE is a British space scientist and science educator who was diagnosed with dyslexia at the age of 8. The passion Maggie had for space led her to read about science, which helped her overcome her dyslexia and begin a career journey. Upon receiving her MBE (Member of the Order of the British Empire), she said, "Imagine a dyslexic from London meeting the Queen of England. It's mind-boggling stuff, but that shows how much potential you have."

Page 14

Abhishek Bachchan

Abhishek Bachchan is a Bollywood producer and actor who has struggled with dyslexia since childhood. He has always been open about his dyslexia and has said that it is important to share his story and promote learning disability awareness. He also had a hand in the 2007 film "*Taare Zameen Par*," a film that follows a young, dyslexic boy struggling through school.

Page 16

Valencia Bioparc, Spain

Bioparc Valencia is an "immersion zoo." Animals do not live in cages but rather in large open spaces and many of the barriers most zoos put in place between different species, including the humans, are either hidden or removed. This 25-acre/100,000-square meter park includes habitats created to represent places like a savannah, Madagascar, and Equatorial Africa.

In Spain, the prevalence of developmental dyslexia among school children is estimated to be between 3 and 6%. This statistic jumps to almost 12% if spelling difficulties are included with dyslexia.

Page 17

The Vancouver Aquarium, Canada

The Vancouver Aquarium opened in 1956 as Canada's first public aquarium. It houses 65,000 animals and is a center for marine research, education, conservation, and animal rehabilitation. The aquarium includes aquatic displays that contain more than 2.5 million US gallons of water.

In Canada, it is estimated that 15% to 20% of the population has dyslexia - about 6 million people. In every classroom there are likely 4 or 5 students who have difficulty reading and writing.

Page 18

Cité de l'Espace, France

The Cité de l'Espace is a scientific discovery center in France focused on spaceflight. It is full of exhibits and hands-on activities that explore France's aviation history and the relationship between Earth and the Universe. There are full-sized replicas of rockets, a control room mock-up, and two planetariums.

In France, 8% of children in grade school have a learning disability. That statistic is made up of dyslexia, dyscalculia, dysorthography, and dysgraphia (trouble with reading, arithmetic, spelling, and writing).

Page 19

Smithsonian National Museum of African American History and Culture, USA

The Museum opened in September 2016 with a ceremony led by President Barack Obama. Part of the Smithsonian Institution, this museum is home to the largest collection of items dedicated to African American history and culture and its influence on American and global values.

In America, 5% to 15% of the population —14.5 to 43.5 million children and adults—have Dyslexia. It is the most common of all neuro-cognitive disorders in the United States and represents 80% to 90% of those with learning disabilities.

Page 21

Greg Louganis

Greg Louganis, one of the world's greatest divers, finally recognized his dyslexia in high school when he was given 'dyslexia' as a vocabulary word. He won a silver medal at the 1976 Olympic Games at age 16 and he won two gold medals in both the 1984 and 1988 Games. And aside from his first Olympic silver medal, he has never lost a competition — including the Olympics, World Championships (where he received the first-ever perfect 10s score), and the Pan-American Games.

Page 22

Ann Bancroft

Ann Bancroft, polar explorer, athlete, and educator, was formally diagnosed with dyslexia as a 7th grader. Bancroft struggled in school, but she managed to get by with help from her parents and tutors. She would become the first woman to cross the ice to the North Pole, traveling 1,000 miles by dogsled. A few years later, she headed an all-woman team to the South Pole, becoming the first female to cross the ice to both the North and South Poles.

Page 23

Justin Wilson

Justin Wilson was a British motorsports car driver. He was tested for dyslexia at age 11 and was formally diagnosed with dyslexia at 13. The racing world became his refuge from his struggles with school. He eventually competed in Formula One racing, the Champ Car World Series, and the IndyCar Series. He often told kids that they have to challenge themselves to work around their dyslexia and not let it limit them.

Sir Lewis Hamilton

Sir Lewis Hamilton MBE HonFREng is a 7-time champion British motorsports driver. He did not realize he suffered from dyslexia until he was 17. Lewis supports the charity campaign TOGETHERBAND, which seeks to provide quality education to all children. He has partnered with, and been made an Honorary Member of, the Royal Academy of Engineering to find ways in which motorsport can engage more young people from Black backgrounds with science, technology, engineering, and mathematics subjects.

Page 24

Joffrey Lauvergne

Joffrey Lauvergne is a French professional basketball player. Lauvergne, who spent several seasons playing in the US and now plays in Europe, struggled with dyslexia as a child. His reading challenges also caused difficulties with writing. Now he enjoys reading, especially history.

Magic Johnson

Magic Johnson is one of the greatest basketball players of all time, a successful businessman, philanthropist, and dyslexic. Johnson struggled with reading and writing during school but being persistent helped Johnson succeed in spite of his dyslexia.

The Author

Keith Magee is a dyslexic public intellectual and political advisor with a focus on social justice, public policy, and public theology. He is Senior Fellow and Visiting Professor of Practice in Cultural Justice at UCL Institute of Innovation and Practice and Fellow at the Centre on US Politics. He is also Chair and Professor of Practice in Social Justice at Newcastle University Law School. He is chair of The Guardian Foundation. He is also the author of Prophetic Justice: Race, Religion, and Politics.

As a dyslexic, Keith's most significant accomplishment is the co-creation of the Multicultural Dyslexia Awareness Initiative at the Yale Center for Dyslexia & Creativity. He speaks as a dyslexia ambassador, and has secured over $15 million to develop global programs and initiatives that advocate for and support people with dyslexia. One such project led to the co-founding of the St. Joseph's University Urban Teachers Masters' of Education Residency Training Program to train teachers to teach dyslexic children to read.

In June 2013, Keith interviewed Harry Belafonte at the launch of the Multicultural Dyslexia Awareness Initiative. Mr Belafonte was the first person the author had ever heard describe dyslexia as a 'superpower'.

The Illustrator

Creative Graphics is a multilingual illustration and design company that has compiled many books and worked for a wide range of clients since it was founded in 1996.

(Website: www.creativgraphics.com)

Acknowledgements

Special thanks to the visionary team Julia Vlock and Joel Campo; editorial Joanne Clay and Edward Weston; research Lila Etter and Ivan Garcia Cuellar; administrative support Tyra Enchill; and the 'expert' consultants Zayden Magee, Jace Myrie, Andre Wilson, and Amauri Wilson.